FAST FORWARD
▶▶3▶▶

OXFORD INTENSIVE ENGLISH COURSES

FAST FORWARD 3

Teacher's Book

PAM EAVES

Oxford University Press 1988

Oxford University Press, Walton Street, Oxford OX2 6DP

Oxford London
New York Toronto Melbourne Auckland
Petaling Jaya Singapore Hong Kong Tokyo
Delhi Bombay Madras Calcutta Karachi
Nairobi Dar es Salaam Cape Town

and associated companies in
Berlin Ibadan

Oxford is a trade mark of Oxford University Press

ISBN 0 19 432309 9

© Oxford University Press 1988

All rights reserved. No part of this publication may be reproduced, stored in a retrieval system, or transmitted, in any form or by any means, electronic, mechanical, photocopying, recording or otherwise, without the prior permission of Oxford University Press.

This book is sold subject to the condition that it shall not, by way of trade or otherwise, be lent, re-sold, hired out, or otherwise circulated without the publisher's prior consent in any form of binding or cover other than that in which it is published and without a similar condition including this condition being imposed on the subsequent purchaser.

Set in ITC Garamond by VAP Group Ltd
Kidlington, Oxford

Printed in Great Britain by Ebenezer Baylis & Son Ltd
The Trinity Press, Worcester and London

Contents

2   **INTRODUCTION**
    Thinking about language learning
    Reading, Listening, Speaking
    Vocabulary
    The Plural Problem: a poem
    Spelling and pronunciation: two poems

5   **UNIT 1**
    Eat, drink and relax
    You are invited . . .
    Party Food
    Relaxation and Inspiration
    Food Proverbs
    Advice through Rhymes
    Tongue Twisters
    English Vines and Wines
    English Pubs

9   **UNIT 2**
    People
    Find Someone Who . . .
    The Lakeland Sheep Farmer
    The Baobab Tree Collector
    What Word am I Thinking of?: a game
    Warning: a poem
    Medical Jokes

12 **UNIT 3**
    Holidays and travel
    Amazing Facts and Figures
    A Narrow Escape from Death
    Kenya Safari
    Planning a Holiday in Kenya: a role-play
    Trials of a Tourist: a poem

16 **UNIT 4**
    The human brain
    The Two Sides of the Brain
    Memory
    How Creative are You?

20 **UNIT 5**
Work

*Work Proverbs
Career Counselling
Job Satisfaction
Life at the Bottom
What's My Line?: a game
The Selection Board: a role-play*

25 **UNIT 6**
School

*Attitudes to Education
The Ideal Teacher
The School that I'd Like
Ask the Right Question: a game
Rural Schools
School Closure: a role-play*

30 **UNIT 7**
Business and industry

*Difficult Tasks for Managers
Brain Teasers
Young Enterprise
Find the Hidden Word: crosswords
Set for Survival
The Wholesome Bread Co-operative: a role-play*

36 **UNIT 8**
Advertising

*The Advertising Standards Authority
Advertising Features
Drive an Ad!
It Pays to Advertise: a poem
Song of the Open Road: a poem
Freedom in a Pie
Describe and Draw: a game
Commad Ltd.: a role-play*

41 **UNIT 9**
Sex and gender

*A Riddle
What Has Sex Got to Do With It?
Sex Stereotyping
Working in a Night-Club
The Gift Game*

45 **UNIT 10**
A taste of literature

*Thinking about Reading
The Collector
Find the Title: a game
On the Bookshelf
The Arts Council Meeting: a role-play
A Short-story Writer: Frank O'Connor*

48 **TAPESCRIPT**

Introductory note

Fast Forward 3 is intended to help advanced students of English to improve their knowledge of the language through the use of authentic material. The Classbook concentrates on the skills of reading, listening and speaking. Grammar exercises – linked with the material in each unit – are provided in a separate Resource Book, as are follow-up writing activities.

Students are encouraged to take a new look at ways of learning and revising vocabulary. The aim of the Classbook is not to teach specific 'advanced' vocabulary but rather to develop the skill of deducing meaning from the context and the effective use of a monolingual dictionary. Good use should be made of monolingual dictionaries and other books of reference in conjunction with the course.

The teacher's role in this course should be to establish a comfortable atmosphere in the classroom so that students can get into conversation with ease. Students should work in pairs or groups as far as possible and should exchange partners and groups regularly. When students are working in pairs and groups the teacher should try to listen in the background and to keep a note of common errors or better ways of saying things which can then be discussed and explained afterwards. The teacher should try not to interrupt students except to ask a pertinent question to keep the conversation going.

Fast Forward 3 is designed for four-week intensive courses or for less intensive courses spread over a whole year. It is also ideal as a basis for communication classes.

Introduction
Thinking about language learning

Reading

- **Consideration and discussion about language learning**

1 Reading texts

Elicit ideas from the students, then list their ideas on the blackboard. Here are some of the types of reading texts that the students may come up with, other than those listed in the Classbook:

- textbooks
- magazines
- newspapers
- cereal packets
- food labels for ingredients and date
- letters
- TV programme guides
- timetables

2 Reasons for reading

Here are some reasons for reading that students may suggest:

- for general information, e.g. newspapers
- for specific information, e.g. brochures, timetables
- for pleasure
- to learn
- to improve their English
- out of idleness and curiosity

3 Ways of reading

Students may mention the following ways of reading:

- scanning
- skimming
- reading for detail

4 Reading in English

Don't be tempted to explain the word 'flick'. Simply perform the action so that the students can follow suit.

Remind students of different reasons for reading and different ways of reading as you work though the material in this book.

Listening

- **Consideration and discussion about language learning**

Students will note among other things that listening is usually more difficult than reading because:
- there is no text in front of them
- they cannot back-track if they haven't understood
- people speak very fast
- different accents may make it hard to understand

Speaking

- **Consideration and discussion about language learning**

Encourage the students to discuss two statements at a time in small groups, while you stay in the background.

Vocabulary

- **Discussion about learning, recording and reviewing vocabulary**

1 Learning new vocabulary

Now discuss the word 'flick' and in particular whether the students *want* to try to remember it.

From now on encourage the students to consider the value of new words before trying to learn them.

2 Recording new vocabulary

Point out how boring vocabulary books with lists of words usually are. Do students really learn from such lists? Get students to compare how each of them records vocabulary.

Suggest the students try different ways of noting new words – particularly combining different senses to include actions, feelings, sounds, pictures and even smells.

3 Reviewing new vocabulary

Encourage students to compare their methods of reviewing new vocabulary and to learn different techniques from each other.

The Plural Problem

- **Reading and listening for pleasure**

The poem is intended for fun; the irregularities of English are usually quite fascinating.

Explain any new vocabulary (e.g. 'brethren', comparing with 'brothers') but discuss with the students the *value* of recording and learning such words as ox, fowl, moose, etc.

Spelling and Pronunciation

- **Reading and listening for pleasure**

1 As well as this exercise, students may also do Exercises 2 and 3 in the Resource Book before attempting the poems.

2 Explain the new vocabulary, e.g. 'bough' and 'dough', and again ask the students if these are words that they *want* to remember, and if so *how* they will remember them.

As an example of one technique for remembering the word 'bough', draw a picture on the blackboard of a bough laden with fruit and, to aid pronunciation ('bough' rhymes with 'cow'), draw a cow underneath it.

Students listen and repeat the poem line by line. Some students can then be asked to read aloud – with expression. Students can also be asked to learn one verse by heart to recite the next day.

3 Listen and repeat before students attempt to recite alone.

1 ▶▶ *Eat, drink and relax*

You are invited...

- **Reading and discussion**

Let students discuss the party invitations in pairs. Point out that they are not going to any of the parties, they are only imagining the situation – therefore use 'would'. Remind students of the use of hypothetical conditions (see Resource Book Unit 4): 'If you *went* to one of these parties, which one *would you go* to?'

See page 9 of the Resource Book for writing practice linked to this section.

Party Food

- **Vocabulary preparation**
- **Topic introduction**
- **Reading for specific information**
- **Guessing meaning from context**

1 Individual work, then discussion in pairs. The 'good stimulants' in the list are (according to the article *Talk and Cheese*):

strong cheese; salted peanuts; potato crisps (if salted!); pickled herrings; chicken liver paté; peppermint chocolate; Coca Cola; coffee; white wine; champagne; tequila (especially if served with salt); sangria; Chianti

2 Students now check their answers to Exercise 1 with the text. Work in pairs again.

3 Students do this exercise without reference to the text. Likely answers are:
1 atmosphere, spirit, *mood*
2 having, giving, organizing, *throwing*
3 party, one, event, *do*
4 be successful, be good, be lively, be wild, go well, *go with a swing*
5 better, more effective, like it/them, *to beat them*

Grammar Exercises 1 (on verb patterns) and 2 (on the pattern verb + object + complement) in the Resource Book may be done after this section.

Relaxation and Inspiration

- **Reading for specific information**
- **Discussion**
- **Learning vocabulary through visualization**

Discuss relaxation and inspiration aids before students read the text. You may include fresh air and exercise, yoga and transcendental meditation among other things. Students may have other ideas.

Ask students to keep notes of all the ideas mentioned. They will need them for the writing task on page 9 of the Resource Book.

Food Proverbs

- **Vocabulary extension**

The use of a good monolingual dictionary or a dictionary of idioms may be useful here.

Advice through Rhymes

- **Reading for pleasure**

Listen and repeat each poem, then discuss the questions. Students can also be asked to learn one of the poems by heart and recite it – with feeling – the next day.

Tongue Twisters

- **Pronunciation and rhythm practice**

Play the recording of each of these tongue twisters in turn. Get students to repeat, emphasizing the importance of speed and accuracy. Play as a game with two teams if suitable.

Don't overdo this exercise – keep it very brief.

English Vines and Wines

- **Topic introduction**
- **Listening for specific information**

1 Students should guess the answers to these questions before listening to the tape. They can then compare their answers with the actual answers (below: see also the transcript on page 48). Students may need to hear the tape two or more times.

1 They enjoyed drinking local wines on holiday on the Continent (in France and Germany). After the holiday they read an article about the possibility of growing vines in England which intrigued and amazed them.
2 They read all the available literature and went to visit vineyards in SE England.
3 2000 vines. (Note: students will probably have guessed a much smaller number.)
4 They looked at six possible sites, and then persuaded a farmer to sell them a piece of land with a south-facing slope and suitable soil for viticulture.
5 Mr Latchford, his wife and children, friends and other people (at harvest time up to 50).

2 Answers:

1 In October/November.
2 150 gallons.
3 1976.
4 Quite good, but not up to 1976.
5 This is his dream, but it will take a long time as there are many problems, particularly the need to find the right variety of grape.

English Pubs

1 Students write down anything they know about or associate with pubs in Britain in not more than two minutes. They then discuss together what they know. Mention of pub opening and closing times could be made here.

2 Ask students to look at the headline of the article and to say what they think it is about. Accept any suggestions students may give, but do not tell them what it is about. Instead, get them to read the article and see if their prediction is right. Then ask them to explain the headline.

3 Students work out together the questions the researchers must have asked in their pub survey.

In Option 1 of the exercise (where students are studying in the UK), the groups report back to the rest of the class. A set of questions should be agreed upon and written on the blackboard by a student or the teacher, paying attention to the grammar and style of the questions. (See the sample questionnaire below.) These questions can then be typed up and photocopied so that students have five or ten questionnaires to use to interview other students, their landlord or landlady, people in pubs or any other English people they may meet. It's a good idea to give students several days or a weekend to complete the questionnaires. Students should then try to summarize their findings and report back to the class.

In Option 2 of the exercise (where students are studying outside the UK) similar questionnaires should be devised about pubs, bars or restaurants in their own country.

Note the writing task on page 9 of the Resource Book linked to this questionnaire.

Grammar Exercises 3 (on prepositional verbs) and 4 (on Present simple and progressive tenses) in the Resource Book may be done after this section.

PUB SURVEY – SAMPLE QUESTIONNAIRE

1 What kind of entertainment do you like most?
2 How many times a week do you go to the pub?
3 Do you have a local?
4 What do you look for in a pub? Rate these things from 1–6 in order of importance:

    comfortable seats   clean glasses
    clean loos   general cleanliness
    friendly bar staff   other (say what)
    quality of beer

5 In a pub do you want most to:

    meet friends?   have a meal?
    make new friends?   listen to music?
    just drink?   other (say what)

6 What do you usually drink?
7 How much do you usually drink?
8 If you drink beer, do you prefer bottled or draught?
9 Is 18 a reasonable age limit for drinkers?
10 What do you think about closing times?

2 ▶▶ People

Find Someone Who...

- **Vocabulary preparation**
- **Oral interaction**

Students do this exercise in a mêlée. The vocabulary of the questions is taken from subsequent sections of this unit, i.e. *The Lakeland Sheep Farmer, The Baobab Tree Collector* and *Warning*.

The Lakeland Sheep Farmer

- **Topic introduction**
- **Vocabulary preparation**
- **Preparation for reading and note-taking**
- **Reading for specific information and note-taking**
- **Discussion**
- **Learning vocabulary through personalization**
- **Vocabulary extension**

1 Students look at the map and find examples of Lakeland words. They should try to guess their meanings and complete the exercise.

Lakeland words	Standard English words
1 dale	a valley
2 beck	a stream or river
3 water	a large lake
4 fell	a mountain, hill or moor
5 crag	a cliff
6 tarn	a small lake

2 Students find Wasdale Head (Ref. E11) and Scafell (Ref. E/D13) on the map. Students look at the photos of Joss Naylor and discuss their impressions of him with a partner. They make notes and report back to the class. A list of the students' impressions can be written on the blackboard.

3 Students read the text and make notes under the same headings as in Exercise 2.

'Alpen' and 'Mars bar' are explained in the text. Other vocabulary you may like to explain includes:

Aga (1.15) – a solid fuel stove kept burning constantly, used for cooking and central heating.
Round Table (1.70) – a charitable organization of businessmen.
News of the World (1.108) – a tabloid Sunday newspaper of the more sensational kind.

4 Students now compare the notes they made while reading the text with the impressions of Joss Naylor they first formed.

Tell the students to keep both sets of notes for use when they do the first writing task on page 14 of the Resource Book.

5 Class discussion.

6 Class discussion.

7 Examples of Lakeland dialect and their standard English equivalents are as follows:

me boots (1.23)	my boots
fells (1.36)	See Exercise 1
the missus (1.55)	my wife
lad (1.89)	young man, boy
nowt (1.110)	nothing

Students should find these words and work out the meanings for themselves. Ask students to find five other new words which they *want* to remember and write sentences including them.

8 Where possible try to match students with a partner they do not know very well and from a different part of the world.

The students interview each other about how they spend a typical day (in their own country if they are studying in the UK). They should not write anything while they are talking in pairs, but should try to make brief notes immediately afterwards on what they have learnt about their partner. They can refer to their partner for clarification.

Students should keep their notes for use when doing the second writing task on page 14 of the Resource Book.

9 Class or group work.

10 Class discussion.

Note that the Grammar Exercises in the Resource Book are all linked to grammatical items found in the Joss Naylor text. They can therefore be done at any point after Exercise 3 above.

The Baobab Tree Collector

- **Topic introduction**
- **Listening for specific information**
- **Discussion**

1 Individual work, followed by class or group discussion.

2 Students listen to Ellen Drake talking and answer the questions. (See also the transcript on page 48.)

1 She was fascinated by them and found them very interesting to look at when she first saw them. She decided to make a different kind of collection – photos of trees – and then people told her interesting stories about them as well.
2 Huge, ugly, peculiar, funny-looking, interesting.
3 God put it in the Congo, in the jungle; the tree objected – it was too wet. God moved it to the Ruwenzari Mountains; the tree objected again – it was too cold. God got fed up, pulled up the tree and tossed it away. It landed upside down in the hot dry parts of Africa, where it is found today.
4 It is said to have 60 different uses. Its leaves, fruit, roots, shoots and seeds can be eaten. The leaves are also useful for medicine. The bark can be made into rope for baskets or thread for clothes. The shell of the fruit can be used as a cup or bowl or made into a snuff-box.

3 Class or group discussion.

See the linked writing task on page 14 of the Resource Book.

What Word am I Thinking of?

- **Vocabulary review**

Warning

- **Reading for pleasure**
- **Discussion**

Medical Jokes

- **Vocabulary extension**
- **Intonation and narrating with creative expression**

See Writing Task 4 on page 14 of the Resource Book.

3 ▸▸ *Holidays and travel*

Amazing Facts and Figures

- **Oral interaction**

Instructions for this information-gap activity are contained in the Classbook. At the end, compare all the scores of the As and Bs, and declare the winner.

A Narrow Escape from Death

- **Listening for specific information and for inference**
- **Report writing based on notes**

Ask the students to discuss together the journeys they have made and any dangerous experiences they may have had on those journeys. Then read the introduction about Christine Anderson.

1 The students now read the notes on page 23 from the point of view of a newspaper reporter who wants to verify his/her information before writing the story.

2 The students listen to Christine's story on tape and first check that the notes on page 23 are correct. The 'mistakes' are:
- Only *one* man died in the attack; the other two were badly beaten up.
- Christine did *not* spend the night on the beach; she went back to her hotel.
- The reason for the murder was probably theft, not a quarrel. (Note also that it is not clear from Christine's account whether or not the Thais who shared the men's cigarettes and hash were those who later attacked them.)

Students should make additional notes of their own as they listen, so that they can then do the writing exercise in Exercise 5.

See also the transcript on page 49.

3 Students compare notes with a partner to check that they have the right information. They may listen to the tape a second or third time if necessary.

Holidays and travel 13

4 Students discuss which adjectives describe Christine and their impressions of her.

5 It may be a good idea to show students examples of newspaper writing so that they can adopt the right style.

Kenya Safari

- **Skim reading and discussion**
- **Reading for gist and reading for inference**
- **Learning vocabulary through personalization and association**
- **Vocabulary extension**

1 Students read the information about the three people and then *quickly* read the article, assessing in pairs whether or not the holiday is suitable for all three of them.

Vocabulary development:

- *Mosquito-proof.* Other words like *waterproof* and *childproof* could be noted.
- Ask students to find out three different meanings of *mug* ('a large cup', as here; a slang word for 'face'; 'to rob with violence').
- Look up the different meanings of *kit*. Discuss all the things that could go into a kit.

2 Discussion in groups of the headline and the impressions it conveys. Individual reading of the article followed by group discussion on whether or not the holiday was a success.

3 Students complete the questionnaire as if they were Keith Jarvey. Encourage them to add fairly detailed comments in the column provided or on a separate sheet. When the questionnaire is complete, students discuss their answers in pairs.

4 Discuss with the students where the text was originally published (in *The Guardian*).

The style of the article makes it most suitable for the 'Travel' section of a daily newspaper or a Sunday supplement such as *The Observer Magazine* or *The Sunday Times Magazine*; it is chatty and very personal, yet informative. A Kuoni advertising brochure would tend to glamorize certain aspects of the holiday and would not include as much personal impression and detail. A scientific magazine about Africa would deal with the geography, location, landscape and vegetation in more technical detail and would perhaps also discuss the wildlife and the issues of preservation and conservation, but would not be concerned with chatting about one person's holiday experiences.

5 Arrange the students in groups of five or six and ask them each to think of a different country that they have enjoyed visiting or would like to visit.

When the students have drawn their columns, but *before* they look at the vocabulary given in the box, encourage them to make associations of their own between the countries and their feelings. It may be best to do this on a fairly simple level at first, e.g. *hot, cold, happy, sad, angry, sunny, damp, honeymoon, prison*.

When the students have understood what is meant by 'association', ask them to try to make associations between the countries in their list and the words in the box. They can then explain their associations to others in their group.

6
1 journey, trip
2 trip
3 travel
4 travels
5 Travel
6 voyage
7 journey, trip

7 Classwork. Ask the students to describe a situation in which they would move as suggested, e.g. as a platoon of soldiers in the jungle ('creep in single file'), as a group of schoolchildren on an outing ('walk in a crocodile').

8
1 The verbs are *snort* and *grunt*. (line 38)
2 A pride. (line 33)
3 horse – neigh; frog – croak; cat – miaow, purr; hen – cluck; cow – moo; dog – growl, bark; pig – grunt; lion – roar; duck – quack; sheep – baa.
4 sheep – flock; duck – XXXXX; cow – herd; elephant – herd; puppies, kittens – litter.

The exercises in Grammar Practice 1 in the Resource Book could be done at this point in the unit. See also Writing Practice 1, 2, and 3.

Planning a Holiday in Kenya

- **Role-play**

Set this role-play up carefully so that half the class are Tourists and half Travel Agents with the appropriate role cards and the information on Kenya for the Travel Agents.

Tourists work in pairs or groups to prepare the questions they want to ask the Travel Agents.

Travel Agents read the information about Kenya and work out anything they do not understand between themselves or with a dictionary. They could also make notes or underline information of particular importance and test that they are familiar with it by asking each other a few questions.

Each Tourist visits a Travel Agent and asks for information. The Travel Agents give advice and make suggestions.

Trials of a Tourist

- **Reading for pleasure**
- **Rhythm and intonation practice**
- **Discussion**

Play the recording of this poem, one verse at a time. Students listen and read, and repeat.

Ask students to imagine incidents when a tourist might use such phrases or to remember when they themselves have had such experiences. They can then tell their stories to the rest of the class.

Grammar Practice 2 in the Resource Book should be done at this point in the unit.

4 ▶▶ The human brain

The Two Sides of the Brain

- Topic introduction
- Vocabulary preparation
- Listening for specific information
- Learning vocabulary through visualization
- Learning about the brain for personal application to language learning

1 Students read the introductory paragraph and then do Exercise 1.

1 verbal – using words to name, describe, define
2 non-verbal – awareness of things, but minimal connection with words
3 spatial – seeing where things are in relation to other things . . .
4 logical – drawing conclusions based on logic . . .
5 linear – thinking in terms of linked ideas . . .
6 synthetic – putting things together to form wholes

2 This listening exercise has two options, one for those who know something of the subject, the other for those who are new to the subject.

The missing labels are:
Left	**Right**
verbal	non-verbal
logical	spatial
linear	synthetic

See also the tapescript on page 51.

3 The *non-verbal* function is being used.

4 Discuss with the whole class the use of illustrations as an aid to memorization.

5
1 to rack one's brains about something – to think very hard or for a long time . . .
2 to pick someone's brains – to talk to someone about a problem . . .
3 to have something on the brain – to think repeatedly . . .
4 to have a brain-wave – to have a good thought or idea . . .

He'd had the tune *on his brain* all day.
He *racked his brain*.
Then he had a *brain-wave*.
Why not speak to John and *pick his brains?*

Memory

- **Oral interaction**
- **Reading for specific information and applying that information**
- **Discussion**
- **Using a monolingual dictionary to explore a semantic field**
- **Vocabulary extension**
- **Vocabulary review**

1 Discuss the idioms with the whole class.

2 Make sure that the students get up from their seats and walk around the class to do this exercise, talking to as many different people as possible.

Also check that they use the correct question forms, either Direct Questions, e.g. *What did you have for dinner last night?* or Indirect Questions, e.g. *Do you remember what you had for dinner last night?*

3 Encourage students to talk about *how* they recalled the things in Exercise 2.

4 A possible definition of 'memory' could be: 'The ability to record life's experiences and to recall some if not all of these.'

5 Discuss which types of memory students used while doing the 'Find someone who . . .' exercise, and which they did not use.

'Collective memory' could be illustrated with these examples: in Saudi Arabia people love to drive out into the desert because they 'remember' a past life as bedouins, living in the desert; in England people get so much pleasure from gardening and having an allotment perhaps because of a 'memory' of living and working on the land in the past.

6 Emphasize to students that they should simply *read* the words in the experiment, not *study* them.

If students read the words quickly without any attempt to learn them, and then write them out in the box on page 39, this should illustrate the primacy/recency effect. But if they study the words and devise a technique to remember them, then primacy/recency cannot be shown.

However, the list *can* then be used to illustrate the importance of vocabulary-learning techniques, e.g. 'sets' of associated words (animals, fruit, etc.). Draw students' attention to this after they have done the experiment.

7 Class discussion of the results of the experiment. Advise the students to make notes on the discussion so that they will later be able to do Writing Practice 1 in the Resource Book.

8 Encourage students to discuss together what they have read about memory and how they can apply this to their learning of English and their learning of any other subject or skill.

There is useful advice in this section for any student wishing to improve his/her study skills. Point out particularly the importance of breaks and changes of activity. (You may also like to check that you apply these ideas in your own teaching.)

Note also the usefulness of the von Restorff Effect for teachers and students. For example, with reference to vocabulary learning, draw funny pictures or write words in funny ways (cf. Units 1 and 2) to help students remember them. Use colour on the blackboard or printing as well as long hand to emphasize a point. Tell funny stories or anecdotes to help students associate words with particular situations. Above all, emphasize the uniqueness of everything.

See Writing Practice 2 in the Resource Book.

9 Provide a class set of monolingual dictionaries or lexicons, or ask students to get their own for use on this and other such exercises in the book.

Look at the dictionary entry for 'memory' together with the students and show them how to check on pronunciation and stress, the different meanings of the words, and common collocations. Collocations they may note are: *within living memory, memory bank* (of a computer), *to have a good/bad memory for dates*, etc.

Let the students look up other words for themselves.

10 Individual work.

Verbs	Nouns	Adjectives
to retain	retention	retentive
to recognize	recognition	recognizable
to impede	impediment	
	episode	episodic
to sense	sensation	sensory
to taste	taste	tasty
	fact	factual
to digest	digestion	digestive
to stand out		outstanding
	gene	genetic
to visualize	vision	visual
to emphasize	emphasis	emphatic

11 Group work or whole class.

How Creative are You?

Discussion

1 Time the students for two minutes as they try to write down as many uses as possible for a paperclip. They may come up with some of these:

to keep papers together
to keep a skirt or trousers done up
to do up a zip if the toggle is broken
as a hair grip
to attach a price tag
to attach an airline bag label
as a bookmark
as a peg for clothes

2 The two faults of the test, which the students should get from reading the test, are:

- it assumed creative ability to be simply quantitative (line 10)
- it did not actually measure 'creativity', but rather the rigidity with which the person tested has been taught to use language, especially words like 'uses' (lines 16–17).

3 A fun exercise. Working in pairs, students try to make connections between a paperclip and the items mentioned. Don't let the activity go on for more than five minutes. Then go through only the most difficult ones, unless the students express a desire to know everybody's ideas.

See Writing Practice 3 in the Resource Book.

5 ▸▸ Work

Work Proverbs

- **Vocabulary extension**

Discuss the proverbs as an introduction to the topic of the unit.

Career Counselling

- **Topic introduction**
- **Vocabulary preparation**
- **Listening for specific information and for gist**
- **Discussion**

1 Individual work, followed by pairwork.

1 scientific — investigating physical and biological phenomena . . .
2 computational — dealing with figures
3 artistic — creating and appreciating . . .
4 persuasive — influencing others . . .
5 practical — working with tools and materials
6 literary — expressing ideas and feelings . . .
7 welfare — concerning yourself with helping others

2 Individual work, followed by pairwork.

1 intellectual — searching for the truth . . .
2 aesthetic — seeking beauty and harmony . . .
3 power — seeking and competing for positions . . .
4 religious — seeking spiritual rather than material satisfaction
5 material — seeking practical means to achieve . . .
6 altruistic — seeking ways of helping other people . . .

Work 21

3 Before listening to the recording, discuss with the students what they think the career-counselling service might have done to find out more about Jonathan and to help him.

1	**Activity**	**Purpose**
1 Occupational interests questionnaire	to find out what sort of jobs he might like.
2 Study of values questionnaire	to find out the way he saw the world and what he thought about things.
3 Aptitude test	to test and score different skills and abilities.
4 Interview	to discuss the results.

2 'Would you like to be a window-cleaner or a waiter in a restaurant?'
'When you walk into a church, do you notice first the beauty or the spiritual quality or the people in it?'
Numerical skills, e.g. Complete the sequence 1,3,5,9. Verbal skills, e.g. Identify the odd word out.

3 Yes, in some ways. He didn't find out much that he didn't already know, but it was useful to have his own impressions confirmed. The psychologist was helpful particularly in ruling out certain jobs.

See also the tapescript on page 52.

4 Class or group discussion.

Grammar Exercise 3 in the Resource Book (on some *-ing* and *-ed* words) may now be done. See also page 26 for writing practice linked to this section.

Job Satisfaction

- **Discussion**
- **Vocabulary preparation**

1 Individual work.

2 Students now add to the list any other factors they can think of. Some ideas they might have could be:
- a challenge
- an interest in the job
- a chance to use your brain and increase your knowledge

22 Unit five

3 Students might now decide how important they consider each factor to be. They should number the factors in order of importance, where 1 = the most important.

4 Pairwork (or small group work).

5 Class discussion. Talk about the ladder drawing and work out the meanings of the two phrases associated with jobs.

See page 26 of the Resource Book for writing practice linked to this section.

Life at the Bottom

- **Skim reading**
- **Reading for gist**
- **Reading for specific information**
- **Discussion**
- **Learning vocabulary through visualization**
- **Using a monolingual dictionary to explore meanings**

1 Students look at the photo of Marian Thiel and the headline of the article and try to predict what the article is about. You should not tell them.

2 Students skim-read the article to find out if their prediction is correct.

3 Students read the article again, quickly, filling in the details on the table as they read:

Marian Thiel	1976	2 years ago	now
Job	SENIOR EXECUTIVE in charge of public relations for fashion house	STUDENT STATE REGISTERED NURSE	Final year of SRN training
Salary	£4,500 plus perks	£90 per month £1,080 a year	£140 a month £1,680 a year
Town	Crewe	London	Congleton

4 Students have to mark the statements T (true), F (false), NS (not sure):
1 T   2 T   3 F   4 NS   5 T

5 Pairwork.

6 Class discussion.

7 Class discussion. Students may also like to consider the situation of nurses in this country and in their own.

8 Review of vocabulary. Remind students of the idea mentioned in Unit 4, Memory: that it will help them to remember a word if they try to visualize it.

1 See if students can remember the ladder picture on page 72 and the vocabulary it illustrates.
2 Ask students to add any further items they can think of to the drawing to illustrate *perks*, and to share their ideas with their neighbours.
3 Students should try to make drawings to help visualize the words and phrases provided. Encourage them to walk around and look at other students' drawings.

9 Dictionary work. A monolingual dictionary will be required.

10 More work with a monolingual dictionary. Students then try to illustrate the meanings of the phrases and sentences in the Classbook with quick drawings.

Grammar Exercises 1 (on tenses), 2 (on open conditions), and 4 (on phrasal verbs with *on* and *off*) in the Resource Book may be done after this section.

What's My Line?

- **Discussion**

A game. Students should play according to the rules set out in the Classbook. Make sure that everyone gets a chance to participate.

This is a good opportunity to practice question forms, so pay particular attention to the way students ask the questions. Questions could include:

Do you work indoors/outdoors?
Can you meet other people?
Is your job in a factory?

The Selection Board

- **Role-play**

Students should work in small groups as the selection board of St Peter's Hospital, Crewe, trying to select a Staff Nurse.

They should read the advertisement and the details about the applicants carefully. They will need to return to page 45 to remind themselves of Marian Thiel's details.

They then decide which of the four applicants should get the job, and report their decision and the reasons for it back to the rest of the class.

It is possible that students will not like any of the applicants and may opt for re-advertising the post!

Check that students understand the meaning of *geriatric*. It may be useful to talk about other hospital departments, e.g. casualty, maternity, out-patients, pathology.

See page 26 of the Resource Book for writing practice linked to this final section.

6 ▶▶ School

Attitudes to Education

- **Discussion**

1 Ask the students to read the survey questions numbers 1–5 and answer them. You may find it necessary to explain the difference between Government and Local Authorities.

2 Students now discuss how they answered each question.

A pocket calculator would be useful to work out the class answers to each question as a percentage. The answers could then be summarized in a number of ways. Here are three suggested methods:

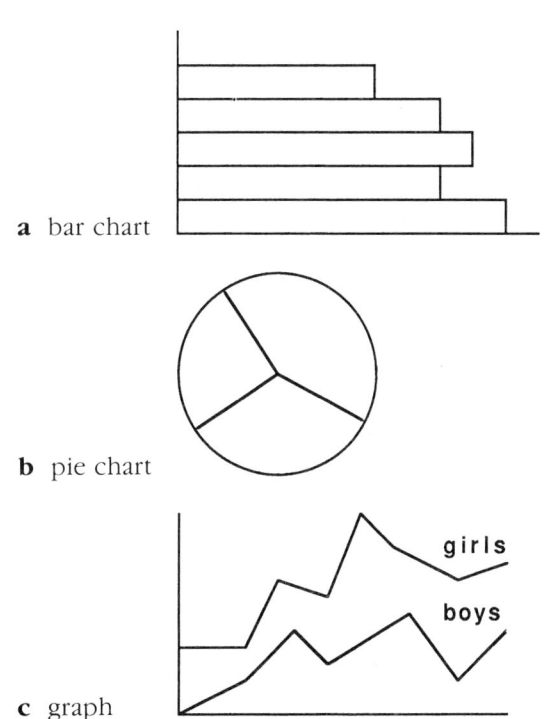

a bar chart

b pie chart

c graph

3 Look at the results of the survey carried out by the *Observer Sunday Magazine*. They are given on page 103. You can now make a comparison of the class survey and the actual results.

N.B. The results in the table in number 5 are out of 300, as the participants in the survey were asked to choose the three most important and the three least important subjects.

See page 30 of the Resource Book for writing practice linked to this section.

The Ideal Teacher

- **Topic introduction**
- **Vocabulary preparation**
- **Listening for gist and for more detailed understanding**
- **Discussion**

1 Individual, then pairwork.

Other attributes students may think of:
- is well-prepared for lessons
- is competent in his/her field
- is able to make a good atmosphere in the classroom
- has the ability to interest pupils
- knows how to win people over
- is a good talker.

Make sure that the students write down their additions to the list.

They compare and discuss their choices of the five most important attributes from amongst those given in the book as well as those they have added.

2 Play the recording of the four teenagers giving their ideas about the ideal teacher. Whilst listening, students note down the attributes that the speakers consider important. Play the tape a second time to give students an opportunity for more detailed understanding. With some classes, this second listening may be unnecessary.

Students then discuss what they have heard and whether they agree with the opinions expressed.

See also the transcript on page 53.

3 Class discussion.

For writing practice linked to this section, see page 30 of the Resource Book.

The School that I'd Like

- **Reading for pleasure**
- **Discussion**

1 To emphasize the differences between the two history lessons cited by William, it is best for the teacher to read out the text. Students then discuss how the lessons relate to their experience of learning history in school.

After discussion, they may like to try acting out the contrasting lessons in small groups.

2 Students discuss the school they'd like or would have liked. This is likely to give rise to quite a lengthy conversation. Appoint a group leader to control the discussion and move the group from one question to another while you stay in the background. Listen and note points to draw the students' attention to later.

3 Students read Melanie's poem and make a list of the changes she would like to make to school. They then compare her ideas with their own, as discussed in the previous exercise.

Grammar Exercise 1 (on participle clauses) on page 27 of the Resource Book may be done after this section.

Ask the Right Question

- **Vocabulary review**

Prepare sets of small cards on which are written words or phrases to be reviewed. Divide students into groups of three or four.

Full instructions for playing the game are given in the Classbook.

For example: | a bully |

Student A What do you call someone who fights other people?
Student B A boxer?
Student C . . . someone who likes to fight people weaker or smaller than himself?
Student B Oh – a bully.

An alternative way of playing this with the whole class would be to have one student, X, standing or sitting at the front of the class, facing away from the blackboard. Write a word on the board and the rest of the class ask questions until X is able to produce the right word.

This game is a very useful way of reviewing vocabulary – and it is fun too!

Rural Schools

- **Topic introduction**
- **Vocabulary preparation**
- **Discussion**
- **Reading for specific information**

1 Students read the list of characteristics of small rural schools. They then look at each one in turn and discuss whether it is an advantage or a drawback, adding others to the list if they think of any.

2 Students read the article on small-scale schools and label each school on the map.

[Map of the British Isles with handwritten labels: PAPA STOUR (Shetland Islands), SUTHERLAND, RHUM (Inner Hebrides), HERM (Channel Islands near Guernsey). Printed labels: Shetland Islands, Orkney Islands, Outer Hebrides, Highlands, Inner Hebrides, Edinburgh, IRELAND, London, Channel Islands Guernsey, FRANCE. Key: × = rural school]

The single most important advantage the pupils in each school appear to have are:

Herm: nature on the doorstep
Sutherland: individual attention/flexibility of timetable
Rhum: wildlife
Papa Stour: flexible timetable (changes of the seasons)

3 Class discussion.

4 Class discussion.

Grammar Exercises 2 (on *it*) and 4 (on phrasal verbs with *out*) in the Resource Book may be done after this section.

School Closure

- **Role-play**

Give students a role and ask them to assume their part by carefully reading their role cards. Try to fit the roles to the people in the class.

With a class of between seven and eleven students, invent some more roles, e.g. other parents or islanders, or even the pupils themselves.

With twelve students, make two groups who can then act out the role-play separately.

With thirteen or fourteen students, give the extra ones different roles, or ask them to chair each group, in which role they introduce the members and lead the discussion.

Make sure the students exploit all the information on their role cards.

The teacher should stay in the background, simply listening to the discussion and noting points to explain or help students with after the role-play is over.

The remaining Grammar Exercises in the Resource Book can now be done. They are numbers 3 (on phrasal verbs with *up* and *down*) and 5 (on present perfect and past simple tenses). There is also further writing practice on page 30.

7 ▶▶ Business and industry

Difficult Tasks for Managers

- **Predicting informational content of a text**
- **Reading for general understanding**
- **Discussion**
- **Using a monolingual dictionary**
- **Vocabulary extension**

Students first look at the cartoon and discuss all the things the employees are doing, e.g. throwing paper darts, making-up, knitting, doing her nails, etc.

1 Students then read the first three paragraphs of the text 'Difficult Tasks for Managers', i.e. just the part of the text that appears on page 58. When they have done so, elicit from them an answer to the question 'What particular aspect of a manager's role do you think the article is about?':
How to deal with difficult employees/ insubordination.

2 Class discussion. Other kinds of behaviour the students may suggest:
- coming to work late and leaving early
- using bad language
- doing their own work instead of the work they are paid for.

3 Individual work. The names should be in this order:
Tactless Ted, Sullen Sally, Familiar Fergus and Cartoon Ken

4 Divide the students into small groups. They discuss how a manager should deal with each of the four problem employees. Having drawn up a table like the one shown in the exercise, they make notes of their suggestions in the left-hand column.

5 Individual work. The names will now be in this order:
Tactless Ted, Familiar Fergus, Cartoon Ken, Sullen Sally

Notes to include in the right-hand column of their table:

	Your suggestions	The author's suggestions
Sullen Sally		Find out her interests and adapt her job or give her more training in what she enjoys. Praise her and show interest in her work. If this doesn't work, put up with her behaviour or give her the sack.
Tactless Ted		Tell him bluntly what a negative effect his comments have on others. Record a staff meeting as evidence. Enrol him on a course in human relations.
Cartoon Ken		Ignore him unless he upsets others. Provide him with more creative work to give positive direction to his talents.
Familiar Fergus		Manager should distance himself from Fergus. Make it clear that special relationships cannot exist. Ultimately, choose between friendship with Fergus and the job.

Finally, students discuss together whether they agree with the author's suggestions.

See page 33 of the Resource Book for writing practice linked to these last two exercises.

6 Individual work. You will need to make sure the students have monolingual dictionaries.

7 Individual work. Expressions used in the sentences:

1 fall on his feet
2 make a clean breast of it
3 turn a hair
4 a pain in the neck
5 keep my hand in

8 Students write some sentences of their own using some of the expressions in Exercise 7, which show clearly what the expressions mean. Blanks should be left where the expressions would be. Other students then complete the sentences.

Grammar Exercises 1 (on modal verbs and the perfect infinitive), 2 (on *should* in future conditions) and 3 (on comparison) in the Resource Book may be done after this section.

Brain Teasers

• **Discussion**

Students work in pairs or groups of three and try to solve the brain teasers. Their solutions can be compared with those of other groups. One or two students may like to explain their solutions on the blackboard to the rest of the class.

Young Enterprise

- **Topic introduction**
- **Reading for specific information**
- **Discussion**
- **Listening for specific information**

1 Students read the short text 'What is "Young Enterprise"?' They must guess the meanings of 'real life' and 'scale-model' from the context.

2 Pairwork. Students should follow the instructions in the Classbook to work out the answers to the questions:

1 The United States
2 1962
3 No, participation is entirely voluntary
4 20
5 Everyone in the company
6 By selling shares
7 A participant in Young Enterprise
8 A practising business executive
9 An ability to get on with young people and an ability to put ideas across
10 An organization which, at its own expense, makes available accommodation, advice and encouragement
11 No
12 The Achievers themselves, with advice from advisers with specialized knowledge in these fields
13 The company goes into voluntary liquidation and reports to the shareholders, declaring a dividend if there is a surplus

Business and industry 33

3 A listening comprehension exercise. Play the tape of the two interviews with people who had been involved in the Young Enterprise scheme. Students listen and answer the questions. (See also the transcript on page 54.)

Interview 1
1 – They meet for two hours a week on the premises of the sponsor company.
  – They decide on the name of the company.
  – They elect a Managing Director, a Company Secretary, and an Accountant.
  – Everyone buys a share at 25p.
  – They choose a board of directors.
  – They decide what products they are going to make, in a brainstorming session.
2 The Advisers try to attend every meeting, particularly in the first three or four weeks of the formation of the company.
3 Problems: Cash flow
  Product
  Product diversification
  Labour disputes
  Market research
  Quality control
4 **a** TRUE (they either show a healthy profit or break even)
  b TRUE (though some have a turnover of £2,000 or £3,000)
  c TRUE

Interview 2
Before listening to this interview, students should draw up a table like the one on page 65 and put into it the main responsibilities they think each of the boys will have had in their company roles.

1 Students now listen and amend the list they made of Josh's responsibilities.

Pause the tape after Josh's first speech to give students time to complete Exercises 1, 2, and 3.

Josh lists his responsibilities as:
– To inform the market of what they were selling and the price, as quickly as possible
– To organize stalls at parents evenings, school fetes, and jumble sales to sell the products
– To make sure enough was sold to keep the company going

2 Students underline in the list the people who bought goods from the company:
teachers, girls at the neighbouring school, friends, parents, Rotary Club members

NB A Rotary Club is a charity organization of businessmen.

3 Students now underline the places where Josh says the goods were sold:
stalls at parents' evenings at school, local shops, school fetes, school jumble sales, local jumble sales

34 Unit seven

4 Students listen as Andrew lists his responsibilities, again amending, if necessary, the lists they made in the table. They are:
- To plan and make the product
- To work out the budget
- To get enough products made for Josh to fulfil his orders
- To get enough supplies in, especially in the winter.

Pause the tape again after Andrew's first speech, to give students time before going on to the next exercise.

5 Now play the part of the interview in which Andrew and Josh say what they feel they have learned from their experience with a Young Enterprise company. As they listen, students should tick the appropriate column in the table beside what each boy says he has learned:

Andrew	Josh	has learned
	✓	how real business works
✓	✓	how to work with others
✓		the importance of good communications
✓		how to handle people
	✓	the jobs different people do in business
✓		how to behave responsibly

See page 33 of the Resource Book for further writing practice.

Find the Hidden Word

- **Reviewing vocabulary through puzzle-making**

1 Pairwork. Answers to the puzzle:

```
        M A R K E T I N G
  S H A R E H O L D E R
        R U N
        E L E C T
V O L U N T A R Y
```

2 Students again work in pairs, this time to make up their own puzzle. They should use 7–10 words that they would like to review from the listening and reading texts in this unit.

Suggestions for the steps to follow are given in the Classbook.

Set for Survival

- **Discussion**

Pairwork followed by groupwork.

1 Students identify in the photograph all the items listed.

2 They now have to suggest an occasion in the office when each of the items would be useful.

3 Pairs now compare their suggestions with those of other students.

When an exchange of ideas amongst a group or the whole class is to take place, it is a good idea to appoint a discussion leader who will control the conversation and encourage everyone in the group to participate. The teacher's role becomes a background one: simply listening to the discussion and noting points to draw students' attention to later.

After discussion, students should read the rest of the text to be found on page 104 of the Student's Book.

The Wholesome Bread Co-operative

- **Role-play**

Read the text which describes what a co-operative is and discuss workers' co-operatives with the whole class.

Explain the role-play situation. The students, in groups, are to be the elected board of directors of the Wholesome Bread Co-operative. They will have to consider various suggestions and problems and decide what action should be taken.

Before the students look at the seven points and try to make their decisions, check that they understand the following items of vocabulary:

compulsory	to be paid on a flat rate
to create differentials	to rotate jobs
leisure hours	to reinvest
the financial year	a crèche
destructive elements	a six-month trial period
to be voted in	

1 Students do the first part of the task on their own. They study each of the points in the text and decide what action they would take. They should write a, b, or c in the column marked 'Your decision' beside each point.

2 For the second part of the task, students work in groups of three or four, acting as the board of directors. Each point is now discussed and a group decision reached, which is then recorded in the second column marked 'The Board's decision'.

The remaining Grammar Exercise 4 (on phrasal verbs with *in*) in the Resource Book may now be done. There is also further writing practice on page 33.

8 ▸▸ *Advertising*

The Advertising Standards Authority

- **Reading for specific information**
- **Guessing meaning from context**
- **Discussion**

1 Students should read the text and answer the questions:

1 To identify and stop misleading advertisements.
2 They have their own watchdogs (teach the word) and they ask the public to inform them of unsuitable advertisements.
3 Students reach their own conclusions after discussing the advertisements.
4 Students should guess the meaning of the expressions from their usage in the text.

Advertising Features

- **Discussion**

Before the lesson collect together a variety of advertisements from magazines, or the complete magazines so that students can find the advertisements for themselves. Suitable magazines would be:

– *The Observer* colour magazine
– *The Sunday Times* colour supplement
– *Good Housekeeping*
– *Cosmopolitan*
– *She*

1 Students look at the list of advertising features and see if they can think of any others. They might suggest:

– Foreign atmosphere
– Purity and goodness
– Health

2 Students divide into small groups to identify which of the features listed appear in the adverts.

You should only allow about 10 minutes for this. Don't let it go on for too long.

3 Class discussion.

Drive an Ad!

- **Vocabulary preparation**
- **Discussion**
- **Listening for specific information**

Look at the picture and introduce the idea of advertising on cars. Buses also display advertisements in this way these days.

1 Read the text. Then, in pairs, students try to *guess* the answers to the quiz.

2 Play the recording of the interview with David Barnes of Poster Motors for students to check how many answers they got right:

1 **c** (only Minis)
2 **a** (£6 a month plus a £10 bonus after 6 months)
3 **a** (all classes of people drive them)
4 **c** (all ages – teenagers to grannies)
5 **a** (introverts – to get themselves noticed)
6 **b** (in Britain and Ireland, though sister companies operate in Europe, and a similar operation is run in the States)

See also the transcript on page 56.

It Pays to Advertise

- **Guessing meaning from context**
- **Rhythm practice**

This is a rhyme to read for pleasure.

1 Students should read the rhyme to themselves and try to guess the meaning of the words *fuss*, *boasts* and *eulogise*.

2 Play the recording of the rhyme for students to listen carefully to the rhythm.

3 Students now recite the rhyme, paying particular attention to the rhythm.

Song of the Open Road

- **Reading for pleasure**

Reading of a poem, followed by discussion of what the poet is complaining about.

Freedom in a Pie

- **Reading for specific information**
- **Learning collocations**
- **Using a monolingual dictionary to explore meanings**

1 Students look at the picture, decide what their reaction to it is, then, by the way they describe the contents of the picture, they should let the rest of the class know what their feelings about the apricot pie are.

2 Students read the first two paragraphs of text and try to answer the questions:

1 He was very attracted by it; it looked tempting and delicious.
2 He was disappointed because although the outside of the pie was like that in the picture, the contents were not.
3 Suggestions for the meaning of *conned* may be tricked, diddled or fooled.

3 Students look at the paragraphs again for examples of the different types of language:

'flowery'   – *a real gem of colour printing*
                  the glow of promise
exaggeration – *a great crusty maw*
                  a torrent of glistening thick syrup
                  great gush of apricot filling
stiff, formal – *Herewith is a packet cover*
language   *I regard this as being a serious deception*

4 Students now read paragraphs 3–9 and fill in the details on the table:

Letters	To	From	Purpose
Paragraph 3	the author	the pie manufacturer	to apologize to put forward a defence
Paragraph 4	the pie manufacturer	the author	to make a complaint to express indignation
Paragraph 5	the author	the pie manufacturer	to put forward a defence to express indignation
Paragraph 6	District Inspector, Weights & Measures Office	the author	to make a complaint
Paragraph 7	the author	District Inspector, Weights & Measures Office	to request further information to describe action that has been taken
Paragraph 8	Peter Jackson, MP	Weights & Measures Office	to put forward a defence to describe action that has been taken
Paragraph 9	Peter Jackson, MP	Parliamentary Secretary, Board of Trade, Mrs Gwyneth Dunwoody	to give further information

Advertising 39

5 Reading of the last part of the text, followed by class discussion.

6 The phrase that refers to the real pie is *a trickle of the stuff*.

7 Other words used to describe the hole where the filling is: *maw, cavern of nothing, hollow*

8 'Dolls up' was originally *dresses up*. 'Dolls up' perhaps implies more the artificiality of the picture of the pie.

9 Students are asked to explain what the Blake quotation means. Undoubtedly they will find this extremely difficult unless they are students of literature, but a possible explanation may be:

The poem says that we can feel the power, goodness and order of the Universe and God in our daily experience and should approach our immediate world with the same wonder as a child who *can* see 'Heaven in a wild flower' and 'Eternity in an hour'.

The author's adaptation of these lines may mean:

Noel Ratcliffe encourages the reader to experience life more profoundly. He draws attention to the material and base motives of the advertising campaign of the pie manufacturers. He compares the 'eternity' of procedure (all the correspondence about the pie) with real eternity and 'the hollow of a crust' with 'the palm of your hand'. He also uses 'freedom' ironically in the sense of the manufacturers making free with reality in the making and advertising of the pie, comparing this with man's freedom to choose his destiny.

10 Work on collocations. Some common collocations of the words given:

a raging torrent	a filled cavity	crusty loaf
a slow trickle	a gaping maw	seductive pose
a yawning cavern	a roaring avalanche	rigid discipline

11 Students work with a monolingual dictionary to find the meanings of the expressions, and then write sentences that illustrate them. Students should leave blanks in their sentences where the expressions should be. Other students then try and complete the sentences.

All the grammar points dealt with in the Resource Book (*should* in subordinate clauses, purpose and result, and phrasal verbs with *put*) will have been met by the end of this section, so the Grammar Exercises may be done at any point after Exercise 5. Writing Practice 1 and 2, on page 36, could also be done at this point.

Describe and Draw

- **Oral interaction**

A game, played in pairs. Full instructions on how to play are given in the Classbook.

Commad Ltd.

- **Role-play**

A simulation. Students should work in small groups in which one person takes on the role of Production Manager, with the rest of the group acting as the production team. They have to produce commercials to fill a five-minute transmission slot. (This could be less, according to the class time available.)

The roles are explained in the Classbook. Make sure the students understand their roles and that they have plenty of adverts to consider. Then let them work together to produce the commercials, while the teacher remains in the background, only offering advice when asked.

Have available a tape-recorder (with microphone if one is not built in) and a blank cassette for recording the commercials.

If a video recorder and camera are available, the commercials could be filmed.

When students have prepared their commercials, they should record them on cassette or video. A useful discussion can follow the playback on the merits of the commercials produced. Production teams can be asked to comment on each other's work. Be careful not to overdo criticism, however. Only a few improvements need to be suggested and favourable comments should be made too.

See also page 36 of the Resource Book for further writing practice.

9 ▸▸ Sex and gender

A Riddle

- **Topic introduction**

Some students will probably see immediately that the surgeon must be the boy's mother, but others will not jump to that conclusion.

When the solution has been found, discuss with the students why it can be difficult to solve such a riddle, mentioning particularly how certain professions have until recently been predominantly male and also how such words as *surgeon*, showing no gender, can be confusing. *Friend* is another such example.

What Has Sex Got to Do With It?

- **Reading for specific information**
- **Listening for specific information**
- **Using grammar reference books**

1 As with other reading texts in this book, students may read silently, aloud around the class, or the teacher may read. Students should then answer the questions:

1 Gender refers to masculine, feminine, and neuter forms of parts of speech.
2 (a) All nouns are either 'le' or 'la', masculine or feminine, but there is no implication of sex in the word.
  (b) There is no gender for the article at all, though there used to be in Anglo-Saxon times.
3 For discussion.
4 Other languages they may suggest: German, Italian, Russian, Spanish.

2

masculine	feminine
actor	*actress*
host	*hostess*
waiter	*waitress*
hero	*heroine*
widower	widow
bridegroom	bride
policeman	*policewoman*

3 Class discussion.

4 *Doctor, surgeon, engineer,* and *chairman* would at one time usually be presumed to be masculine, and *nurse* and *secretary* feminine, but such stereotyping is slowly disappearing, so your students may well have different ideas.

Chairman is a word that is subject to a great deal of controversy these days, when a woman is the leader of a group. Some people prefer to use the alternative 'chairwoman', others use 'chairperson' or 'the chair'.

5 Listening comprehension. (See also the transcript on page 57.) Students must try and complete the sentences with the appropriate pronoun *before listening*. Either let them do this on their own or ask them to call out what they think is the right answer in each case. Several different answers are likely to be given. Do *not* be tempted to tell them which is correct but draw attention to the fact that different possibilities have been suggested.

The correct pronouns are:

1 her
2 she
3 She
4 it
5 they

Other examples of unusual pronoun use:

- Look at *him*, crawling along there. *He's* looking for some food. (of a cockroach)
- Robert ignored me all the evening, and then *it* finally asked me to dance. (of a girl's boyfriend)
- Look at *it*! Have you ever seen such a mess! (woman of her son)
- *It* spoke. (of a quiet person amongst a group of friends who finally has something to say)

Discuss the effect of such usage.

The alternatives to replace *he* are:

he or she   hem   co.
s/he   shay   mon
they

Discuss which alternative is likely to survive in the long term. *They?*

6 Make sure students have an appropriate grammar book for this exercise.

Sex Stereotyping

• **Discussion**

1 Class discussion.

2 Division of the words and phrases could be:

Boys: Boys will be boys
          A little devil*
          A good sport*
          A cry-baby*
          Sensitive*

Girls: Bossy
          As pretty as a picture
          How sweet!
          A little angel*
          A tomboy
          Aren't you adorable!

Those marked * could be either in certain circumstances.

3 Individual work, followed by groupwork and discussion.

See page 40 of the Resource Book for further writing practice linked to this section.

Working in a Night-Club

- **Reading for specific information and reading for inference**
- **Talking about something that you have read about**
- **Using a monolingual dictionary to explore meanings.**

1 Class discussion.

2 Before students read the article, you may like to pre-teach some of the vocabulary from the text. Alternatively, it could be discussed afterwards.

dressed with fashionable androgyny (paragraph 5) – unisex, or having the appearance of both sexes
up from the provinces (paragraph 6) – in London for the glamour to escape the quiet life in the countryside
transvestite (paragraph 6) – a man who has an abnormal desire to dress in women's clothes
à la Boy George (paragraph 6) – in the fashion of the pop singer Boy George who used to dress as a girl
a freak (paragraph 7) – someone abnormal or an oddity in society
to get chatted up (paragraph 10) – to engage in flirtatious conversation
a crash course (paragraph 11) – a very quick and intensive course

You may also wish to discuss the clothes worn by Graham in the picture: *a blonde wig, stiletto heels*, to comment on *à la* with reference to Boy George, and to talk about the meaning of *As soon as I can't carry this off, I'll stop* (paragraph 18).

Students read the first two paragraphs of the article, and discuss what the article is about:

A man who dresses as a woman to be a waitress in a night-club.

3 Students should now read the rest of the article.

The experiences that Graham has had that have made him more sympathetic to women are:

Paragraph 4 – Graham gets harassed at work and learns what to say and how to laugh it off.

Paragraph 10 – People see his long hair and his outfit and assume he's female so he gets chatted up: *If men see a blonde they don't expect any intelligence.*

Paragraph 11 – Graham says: *You learn when to laugh, when not to. You have to be more modest if you're a girl. You tend to let men hold the conversation and you just return it. You give opinions, but you don't hold them too strongly – you tend to take second place to a degree.*

4 Class discussion. David Thomas, the author, seems to take a neutral, very 'straight' attitude to Graham Flander. He simply tells the story from Graham's point of view without making any judgements.

5 Class discussion.

6 Class discussion.

7 Class discussion.

8 Work with a monolingual dictionary, followed by sentence-making.

9 Class discussion.

Grammar Exercises in the Resource Book deal with direct and indirect speech, *used to do* and *used to doing*, verbs with *get*, and *wish*. Any of these may be done after Exercise 4 in this section. There is also writing practice on page 40 linked to this section.

The Gift Game • Oral interaction

A game. Full instructions on how to play it are given in the Classbook.

10 ▶▶ A taste of literature

Thinking about Reading

- **Topic introduction**
- **Discussion**

1 Class discussion of the quotation by Sir Francis Bacon, and books.

Dr Zhivago is a well-known 'book of a film' that some students may have read.

Some examples of a 'film of the book' could be: *Death on the Nile*, *Murder on the Orient Express* (and other Agatha Christie books), *1984* (by George Orwell, starring Richard Burton), *The Thornbirds* (Colleen McCullough), and *The Grapes of Wrath* (John Steinbeck).

The Collector

- **Reading for pleasure and reading for specific information**
- **Guessing meaning from context**

If possible bring to class copies of *The Collector* and *The French Lieutenant's Woman*.

1 Skim reading of the publisher's blurb on the back cover of *The Collector*. Encourage students to read quickly as they might when browsing through books in a bookshop or library, and not to worry about understanding every word. They should simply assess whether they would enjoy reading the book.

2 Students read the text, which is two extracts from different parts of *The Collector*, one from the point of view of 'The Collector', the other from the captive's diary.

3 Encourage students to reflect on their impressions of the characters and the stories and to answer the questions:

1 Frederick asked Miranda to help him with a dog he had run over, suggesting it was in the back of his van. It was just a story. When she peered into the van, he overpowered her with a chloroformed pad and when she lost consciousness, he got her into the van. It seems he had carefully planned this because he knew exactly when to expect her and where to wait and he had the chloroform ready and a bed in the back of the van.

2 It gives the sentence great emphasis. We know Miranda is now in Frederick's control.
3 *cunningly worked suspense*
 ... tension and pathos are equally blended
4 It seems to be a cell – perhaps in a basement or cellar: *down here*; it's made of stones but very firmly cemented as she can't find any loose ones. The door is very solid – made of wood and metal-lined on the inside.
5 D and M could well be Daddy and Mummy or else a married couple she knows well. G.P. is probably someone older, perhaps a college lecturer or a teacher, whom she admires. (Some students may confuse G.P. with *a* G.P. – a General Practitioner – so draw attention to the use of the indefinite article or lack of it.)
6 She has begun to turn inwards and to think very hard about herself and her life.
7 Let the students discuss this.
8 Let the students speculate but if they insist on wanting to know the truth: Miranda dies; she falls ill and fades away after a failed escape attempt.

4 Draw the students' attention to the colloquial style of the two extracts and ask them to try to work out for themselves the meaning of the phrases.

In the Resource Book there are Grammar Exercises on *as if*, *as though*, relative clauses, phrasal verbs and prepositional verbs, and unreal past conditions. Any of these may be done after this section.

Find the Title

- **Oral interaction**
- **Learning about books for extensive reading**

1 A game. The instructions are in the Classbook, as well as the 'answers' (page 105).

Try to bring some of these books, or others by the same authors, into class for the students to browse through and to read if they choose. Try to foster a desire to read English for pleasure as much as possible.

2 Discussion in pairs.

On the Bookshelf

- **Discussion**

1 This is fun. The titles of the books on the left relate to the name of the authors on the right. Students try to match the titles with the most appropriate names.

A taste of literature 47

Look at the example together: Rice Growing by Paddy Field. Explain how Paddy Field can be both an Irish name and a phrase to describe an irrigated field for growing rice.

Advise students to say the authors' names aloud and to let their imaginations play with the words. Answers:

2   The Burglar by Robin Banks (a pun on 'robbing banks')
3   Home Heating by Arthur Mometer (= a thermometer)
4   The Cannibal's Daughter by Henrietta Mann (= Henry ate a man)
5   On the Beach by C. Shaw (= seashore)
6   Keeping Cheerful by Mona Lott (= moan a lot)
7   A Cliff-Top Tragedy by Eileen Dover (= I leaned over)
8   Try Again by Percy Vere (= persevere)

2 If students enjoy doing these, let them try making up their own titles to go with the authors given. Here are some possibilities to share with the students if you like:

Germ Warfare by Mike Robe
The Cold Dessert by I Scream
Stiletto Heels by R U Short
A Guide to Insomnia by Eliza Wake
Motorway Madness by Laurie Driver
A Cold Wind by I C Blast
The Sting by Amos Quito

The Arts Council Meeting

- **Role-play**

Make sure that students understand the situation. Allot roles and tell them to read their instructions carefully, but not to read anybody else's. They can then hold the meeting of the Arts Council, working through items on the agenda.

A Short Story Writer: Frank O'Connor

- **Listening to a story for pleasure**

Encourage the students to sit back and listen to the story *without* reading the text. It is for pure enjoyment.

Tapescript

UNIT 1

ENGLISH VINES AND WINES

Marion: Could I ask you, why you started growing vines?

Mr Latchford: Well er, first of all we went to, had a number of holidays in er, on the Continent, Europe, in Fr, France and Germany mostly, and we had er many an interesting time drinking their local wines, and er this time, after returning our, from our holiday in er 1970, we er read this article, which was the er local farmers' er weekly, published in Britain, and er it stated that vines could be grown in England, and also that it could be made a commercial proposition. So er, we were very intrigued by this and er absolutely amazed that they could be grown here. So we er set about er reading all the available literature, and er, which was very limited, at that stage, and, er we found that er quite a number of people had taken up this enthusiastic er pastime, and er, and they were indeed considering making it a commercial proposition. And er so we arranged to visit various vineyards around south-east England, and we enjoyed the, the talk and the, the excite . . . excitement of this new-found er venture. And er so er, we decided that we would er buy some vines er from er Germany and indeed we ordered er two thousand vines and, er at this stage we thought, 'Well, where are we going to grow them?' and er, so we live in quite a, an open agricultural area so we thought it would be quite er simple to obtain a small piece of land to grow these vines, and of course er we set about er looking up the map of this area and er we decided that er, and pinpointed about er six different sites that would be suitable, with a nice south-facing slope, and er suitable er soil. And so we er, we found one eventually, er which is this site here, and er we also found the owner and approached him and said, 'Well, can you sell us a, a few acres of your little south-facing field?' So, he er, after a lot of persuading said he would. And er, he said that he would er sell it to us in the spring. And er, spring came along and we, we, it was er March, and er, we set about, with all haste to er plant these two thousand vines, which was a colossal undertaking, as we discovered as we went along.

Marion: Is it just you and your wife working in the vineyards?

Mr Latchford: Y, yes, er and our children have helped and we've got a number of friends who help and er, certainly at harvest time. Er, we've had as many as fifty people here in harvest time. And er we have a, usually, choose a nice warm sunny er, sunny morning in October, at the end of October, or maybe November, and we er, pick away and usually, um, if we're lucky, we manage a ton, and that is quite sufficient to er press er about a hundred and fifty gallons of juice. The best year we ever had was 1976, which was an absolutely wonderful year, and er we produced two tons from two and a half acres.

Marion: And what are the prospects for this year?

Mr Latchford: It's looking quite good er, possibly not quite as much as in 1976, but we more, we have more vines anyway, we've planted more since then.

Marion: And do you see the day when you could give up your present job in town and move out here and become a full-time vine-grower and earn your living?

Mr Latchford: That is my dream, yes, [laughter] but er, it will be a long time hence, er because er, we do have a lot of er, um well problems, I was saying, and we have to find the perfect, or nearly perfect variety, to grow before we will increase further.

Time: 4' 40" (approx.)

UNIT 2

THE BAOBAB TREE COLLECTOR

Marion: Ellen, what made you decide to write a book about baobab trees?

Ellen: Well, it wasn't something that just er started er suddenly. I think it started a long time ago, er, when I first came to Africa er, and I saw the first baobab tree I'd ever seen in my life and er I was fascinated at this huge, ugly, funny-looking, peculiar, interesting tree. Er, and er, so I, well I just became interested in them, every time I saw them, they, they, they all look different, er from each other and er and I never really got tired of seeing them. And then I decided um, other people have got collections of things, you see, er, some people collect stamps and some collect postcards and some collect, well what have you, I don't know, and er I didn't have a collection of anything and er so I decided, 'Well, I'm going to be different, I'll have a collection of baobab trees.' Now obviously I couldn't collect the trees themselves and er so I decided to collect photographs of them, so I went around, er, taking pictures of these peculiar-looking monsters and er, from that I got more interested in, in them and er, well I talked to some people who told me some interesting stories about them and er, so I decided maybe there was enough to write a book about. So I went then from, from that idea, I started er asking people questions about baobabs, did they know anything about them? Were there any folk tales about them? And the more questions I asked the more encouragement I got that this was a good idea because um, apparently there are a lot of folk tales and a lot of legends and, and stories about particular individual baobabs and er . . .

Marion: Can you tell me any stories about particular baobab trees?

Ellen: Yes, er, er, well, there's one, there's one story which is, is er quite widespread, um, er, all over Africa, and that is that the baobab is, is an upside-down tree, it's not a, er, it's not growing right side up, its, its roots are sticking up in the air and the top of the tree's in the ground. Now . . .

Marion: So you mean, it's, it's called the upside-down tree?

Ellen: It's called the upside-down tree, yea. And er, the reason for this, well there are, there are various stories that er, er connected with why, you know, this happened. But one story which I heard when I was in Kenya, er says that er in the beginning er God, when God was creating the world and, and er putting everything in its place er, God made the baobab tree and planted it I think in the Congo basin or somewhere, where, in the, in the tropical rain forest, and the baobab tree didn't like it there, it was too hot and humid. And so it complained that it didn't, it didn't like the climate and, 'Please it's too wet,' you know, 'There's too much rain and I don't like this.' So God picked it up, pulled it up and put it up in the Ruwenzori mountains, in, the ones that are on the border between Uganda and the Congo I guess, er, and er, put it up there in the mountains. So the baobab complained again, 'I mean, it's too cold, I don't like it, I mean this, this is terrible, you can't, I don't want to stay here.' So God got fed up you see, this tree is complaining all the time, so He just pulled it out and tossed it sort of casually, without even paying any attention where He threw it I think, and maybe tossed it over His shoulder, and it landed er upside down er in the hot dry parts of Africa where it has grown ever since. [laughter]

Marion: And is it a useful tree? I mean do [Yes] people [Yes] use it for things?

Ellen: It's very useful. Um, I was told the other day by a botanist er that it's it's the, it's the plant, the one, the only, the one plant that he knows that has the most uses of any other plant. Er, it, as far as I know has, has at least sixty different uses. Er, some of those include, well, it's used, there are a lot of different parts of it that are eaten by people or animals. Er, the leaves can be eaten, they make a good er kind of spinach or, er that you can put them into soup and um, I have actually eaten them and they taste a bit like spinach, kind of, they're kind of slimy but er, er not bad-tasting. Er the roots can be eaten. The er the growing shoots can be eaten. Er, the fruit can be eaten. Er, the seeds can be eaten. Er and then there are er very very many uses er for medicine. Er, the leaves, again, the leaves, the fruit, the seeds, all all the different parts have got er, er uses, medicinal uses. Er, the, the bark is er er kind of stringy and so you can peel the bark off the tree, and er pound it I think so that the fibry, the the fibre parts come loose, and the crumbly bits fall off and er then people make rope and string and so on out of it and then from that string they can weave baskets or they can weave clothing or whatever, what have you. Er, the fruit, er the fruit is er, it's not a soft mushy fruit, it has a, a hard shell like a gourd, so the the hard shell can be used, er for a number of different things, carrying water like a cup, or er or like a, well, yea a cup or a bowl, er, apparently in some parts of West Africa they make snuff boxes out of them, out of the the fruits.

Time: 6' 20" (approx.)

UNIT 3

A NARROW ESCAPE FROM DEATH

Interviewer: How did you come to be in Thailand in the first place?

Christine: Oh, um, I'd been working in New Zealand, travelling overland, you know, I was going from New Zealand to England, um on local trains and buses and things like that. And, when I was travelling through Malaysia to Thailand I came across this little village, very near the Thai border. It was quite late at night so, I thought I'd take a local train to a seaside resort I'd heard about.

Int: In Malaysia?

Girl: No, Thailand, it was right on the border. So, I got on this train, and um, there were these three blokes on it, Canadian, (and) an English, and um, can't remember what the other one was, possibly an Australian or a New Zealander?

Int: Mhm.

Girl: And they were all travelling together. They'd met up in another country.

Int: Were they travelling back to England as well?

Girl: One was going to India; I think the other two were possibly going to England. Anyway I just got chatting to them, they seemed nice. And, er I said, 'Where are you going to stay in this town?' Oh, it was called Patthaya, it was quite a, a big tourist centre now, but then it was just one hotel. And they said, 'Well, we're, we're staying on the beach.'

Int: [laughter] On the beach?

Girl: Well, I, I thought it was a bit risky but I didn't like to sort of say anything about that.

Int: Oh. Why not?

Girl: Well, you see, I'd heard that there were groups of local people who attacked anyone on the beach and, and they got their money stole(n), that sort of thing. So er, even though there were these three big guys, I thought, 'I, I'm not risking this, I'm going to go and get a cheap room somewhere.'

Int: Ah!

Girl: So, I just went into the town and found there were one or two cheap places. They weren't very clean, but they were OK. So I thought, 'I'll go down to the beach and see if they've set up a camp there.' So, later on I, I'd settled in my room and I wandered down, having had something to eat. And um, they'd got all their gear laid out on the beach, they were settling in for the evening – it was about 6 or 7 – and I sat down and chatted to them, um and I went for a, a coffee with the English guy, he was quite nice, and it was getting a bit late, and the other two were still on the beach, and er, this group of Thais came up, and they were all sort of passing round cigarettes and biscuits and things, and everybody seemed to be getting on fine just chatting. And then um, someone got some hash out. And the, the Thais joined in passing it round, everybody seemed fine. So the English guy went back, um and said, 'What are you gonna do, stay here? You'll be all right, (there)'s three of us here.' But somehow I just didn't like the look of the way things were going, erm, with those Thais it's so difficult to tell what, what they're thinking. But um, the three guys, a, w, were pretty stoned by the time I left. I felt there was something wrong and I went back to the hotel. We'd vaguely arranged to meet on the train to Bangkok the next day. There was only one train. Um, the next day I got to the station, and I was the only European! 'That's funny,' I thought. 'Where are they? What's happened to them? Perhaps they've overslept, recovering from the night before?' And I went on to Bangkok.

Int: Yes.

Girl: Well, people when they do these overland routes they get to know about places where to stay through other people, through other Europeans and they sort of swop stories and everything. So I went on to this place and it was mainly students, Europeans . . .

Int: Er, a hotel, a hostel?

Girl: Yeah, sort of, sort of cross between the two, you know.

Int: Mhm.

Girl: It was, erm, a private hotel but it was cheap and there was a swimming pool, and it was quite comfortable and, I spent about a week there, and towards the end of that week I was going into the cafeteria, and there was this, erm, article from a newspaper on the noticeboard.

Int: In English?

Girl: Yes, in English. It was probably from one of the Americans who live in Thailand, th, they publish a newspaper there, and it was about these three blokes that had been on the beach in that village that night.

Int: The same three blokes?

Girl: The same three blokes! They'd been attacked by a group of Thais!

Int: Gosh!

Girl: One of them had been beaten over the head with a club and he'd died from his injuries and the other two were very, very badly beaten up. One was critically ill in hospital and the other had managed to get away and raise an alarm. And the Thais had threatened them and said, 'We want all your money, if you don't give it to us we're going to attack you.' And the three blokes of course stood up to them. And um, I mean they're not very big people, naturally, and they'd set on them with sticks and whatever they could get hold of and, well, one of them had died so, I really had a, a narrow escape from death.'

Int: (You) certainly did!

Time: 3′ 50″ (approx.)

UNIT 4

THE TWO SIDES OF THE BRAIN

Marion: I would like to say a few words about the two sides of the brain, of the human brain, and the functions of these two sides or two hemispheres. Erm, The fact that the brain is divided into a left and a right half is not a new, not a new thing. If you remove the skull then it's quite clear to the naked eye, and this division is true of all animals. What is special about man is that each half has specialized functions. The most obvious difference in functioning is what is known as the crossover effect, that the left hemisphere controls the right side of our bodies and vice versa, that the right hemisphere controls the left side of our bodies. This crossover effect is something that's been known for a long time, um, the ancient Egyptians for example knew that injuries on one side of the brain caused paralysis on the other side of the body. And um at the beginning of this century it was known that damage to certain areas of the left hemisphere resulted in things like the loss of speech or in poor reading, showing that the left hemisphere controlled our verbal abilities. Damage to the left hemisphere um also can cause um general deterioration in logical thinking, showing that the left hemisphere can um, has a logic, logical function. And um, damage to the right hemisphere could lead to deterioration in visual and spatial functions, so that for example, um, someone might have problems in recognizing faces or in dressing himself. But the real breakthrough in our understanding of the functions of the two hemispheres has come in much more recent years, and particularly with the experiments of Roger Sperry and others at the California Institute of Technology since the 1960s. Now, they conducted experiments with epileptics, and with these epileptic patients the corpus callosum, that's the thick nerve cable that, er connects the two halves of the brain, this corpus callosum had been cut and so the patients had split brains, and in fact the experiments are often referred to as the split-brain experiments. Um, and to give you two examples, many many experiments were carried out, but um, two examples. A patient, the, the scientists showed that if a patient was given something to hold in his right hand he could say what he was holding because the information was going to the left side of his brain. But if the object was in his left hand he couldn't describe it, he could only make a guess. But later he could point to the object again with his left hand and, showing that the right half had both recognized the object and had remembered it. Another interesting finding was that, although the right hand er was still, after the splitting of the brain, the right hand was still able to write, which is what one would expect because er verbal ability is located in the left hemisphere, but the right hand lost the ability to draw pictures. And with the left hand the opposite was the case. The left hand couldn't write at all but it could still draw cubes and simple shapes. Other experiments have shown that it seems to be the left hemisphere that is specialized in a kind of linear processing of information, of analyzing information one bit after another, while the right hemisphere specializes in a parallel processing, in taking several bits of information together and forming from them a synthesis. So it seems that each one of us has a double brain with two ways of knowing. Each of our hemispheres gathers in the same sensory information and processes it in different ways, handles it, handles the information in different ways. The task may be divided between the two hemi, hemispheres, each handling the part that suits it best, or sometimes one hemisphere may dominate the other, very often the left hemisphere dominating the right, and will take over and the . . ., inhibit the other half. Now it seems to me obvious that all of us as, as human beings, as individuals, wishes to maximize the use that we make of our brains and I think that this means achieving a balance, a harmony between the two hemispheres, not allowing one to dominate at the expense of the other. And, before I finish I would like just to mention two ways in which I think we can do this, and it relates to two developments that have been taking place, particularly over the last decade or so. Um one way that can help I think is meditation and there has been widespread growth of interest in meditation in recent years in the western world. Um, one technique that you're perhaps familiar with, you may even have tried it for yourself, and that is Transcendental Meditation. And quite a lot of research has been done on people who practise in Transcendental Meditation, and the research has shown that while people are practising this technique the two sides of their brain appear to be functioning together, they appear to be being brought into balance with each other and communicating with each other. And the, the other way that can help I think is education, um, education focusing more on developing the actual skills associated with the right hemisphere, because traditionally in education it is the left hemisphere that has dominated and dominated at the expense of the right. So I think these two approaches, the educational approach and the meditation approach, are complementary and that the best results can be achieved by following them both up. The first one, the meditation, increases the brain's efficiency, while the other, the educational approach, improving the skills associated with the right hemisphere, will allow us to use that increased efficiency, er use it more efficiently still.

Time: 7' 50"

UNIT 5

CAREER COUNSELLING

Marion: Recently you went to a career counsellor. Could you tell me what happened there?

Jonathan: Yes. In fact, before I went they sent me two questionnaires to complete. One of them was to look at my occupational interests, that is what sort of jobs I might like, and the other questionnaire was to look at, was a, a study of values, that is the way I saw the world and what I thought about things. I'll talk about the Occupational Interests questionnaire first. On that questionnaire there were lots of questions, I think forty or fifty, and each question I had to make a choice between two jobs and I had to choose one of them even if I didn't really want either of them, for example, in one question it might say 'Would you like to be a window cleaner or a waiter in a restaurant?' and although I don't really want to be either I had to choose one of them, although in the other questions there was often a much more obvious and easy erm choice to make. And on the basis of those answers they then classified my occupational interests in different categories, for example whether I was interested in, in a job that was scientific, research or something like that, or whether I was more interested in a job which had a welfare aspect to it, helping other people, perhaps social work. The other categories were Artistic, Literary, Computational, working with numbers, Practical, working with tools and materials, and also Persuasive, whether I wanted a job in which I had to persuade and influence others to accept my ideas or my goods and services. So that was the Occupational Interests questionnaire. The other one that I had to complete before I went was called a Study of Values in which I was asked a series of questions about how I felt in certain situations, for example, one question might be 'When you walk into a church do you feel one of the following?' and I had to choose them, I had to make a choice of one out of the following, for example 'Would the first thing I noticed be the beauty, the architectural beauty, or would it be the spiritual quality and atmosphere, or would it be all the other people in the church?' And in this way they, on the basis of this and other questions, they would classify me according to whether my values were more intellectual or aesthetic or material or oriented towards power. And this was a way of really finding out how I saw the world, whether I was more interested in seeking (the) truth through academic investigation, or whether I was more interested in competing for positions of power and authority, etc.

On the day itself we all had to do an aptitude test in the morning. That took about two and a half or three hours and it had several sections in it and each section was designed to test different skills and aptitudes, for example verbal skills, numerical skills, perceptual, mechanical, working with shapes, working with detail. For example in the numerical section, which took about fifteen or twenty minutes, there were fifty or sixty questions, although nobody was expected to answer all those questions but you had to answer as many as you could in that time, and the questions were all of a certain kind, although they became very quickly much more difficult. For example in the numerical section it would start off with a very easy one, with a series of numbers, for example 1,3,5,7,9 and you had to complete the sequence, which in that case would be 11,13,15, but then the questions became much more complicated. In the verbal section there'd be similar questions where you had to identify the odd word out, for example, there might be five or six animals, most of which had two legs but the odd one out would be a cat which had four legs. But again, very quickly the questions became more complicated than that. And then on the basis of, of all those, um, questionnaires, they worked out my score and gave me a score um in terms of whether I was above or below average compared with another person, or other people of my age, and they gave me a score for these different skills, um, verbal, numerical, perception, shapes, mechanical, and detail.

Marion: (Yeah) And did you meet a psychologist or anything or was it just a question of doing tests?

Jonathan: No, in the afternoon I met a psychologist, after they had worked out my results for all my questionnaires, for all the answers I had given to the questionnaires, I met a psychologist who had the results with him and we discussed both the results that the questionnaires had generated and also any personal um feelings that I might have about my career and interests.

Marion: And did anything useful come out of all this for you?

Jonathan: Yes, in some ways it was helpful. I don't think I found out too much that I didn't already know. But it was certainly very useful to have some of my own personal impressions supported or confirmed by a, another method. Um and what I, what I found out was that in certain areas I have particular strengths both in terms of aptitude and interests and the way I see the world, and there are other areas I have certain weaknesses and I should certainly take those strengths and weaknesses into account when choosing another job.

Marion: And was the psychologist fairly specific to you as to what alternative jobs might be suitable for you, based on the results and based on his conversation with you?

Jonathan: Oh, yes. He, he was very specific, both in terms of what jobs might be suitable for me and also what jobs may not be suitable for me. And probably I found the latter more helpful in as much as he identified certain jobs or occupations that certainly would not seem to suit me, which in fact I've, had already considered was the case anyway.

Time: 5' 50"

UNIT 6

THE IDEAL TEACHER

Laura, Nicola and Tracey all live and go to school in Reading. Jillian, who is Tracey's elder sister, has left school and goes to Reading Technical College. They talked to Marion about what they think of their teachers. Marion first asked Laura how she thought a person had to behave in class if he or she wants to be a good teacher.

Laura: Firm but kind and not too, too strict or anything, but you have to be firm I think, but you have to have a nice nature as well, to get on with the pupils, because there are difficult pupils and things in every school, and I think if you've got the right, um, touch, and things like that you can get on with them, even though they may be school bullies or something like that, you've got to have a good nature.

Marion: What do you think are important qualities in the good teacher?

Nicola: Well, I think that teachers ought to be able to control the class and that they needn't have any pets, like tell them that they haven't got any favourites, because our maths teacher didn't have any favourites, and he was strict on us and we got on well in our maths. But in some lessons the teachers are young and they're not so strict and we don't do much work really. And um we think that the maths teacher is the ideal teacher.

Marion: What about you?

Tracey: Um, the teachers I find I get on best with are the fairly young teachers, the, the ones with a sense of humour so they can keep the lesson lively, because some teachers just burble on and it gets really boring. If they can have the occasional joke, but, you know, if they're just human teachers and the ones that aren't too strict or too soft. Um, there's quite a few teachers like that at our school, the ones with a slight sense of humour so you don't always feel you're under pressure to be sensible all the time. [laughter] [Yeah, erm.]

Laura: People say that teachers aren't human and all that, but, um, and most, some of the teachers are a bit strict and they never seem to laugh or anything, but I think a sense of humour is ever so important because I mean everyone's got a sense of humour somewhere, and um, I think it brings out the good nature in you and helps to get on with the class.

Jillian: Discipline is very important and a sense of humour but the teacher should also not look down on the pupil. It restricts what you're doing and you, if you don't feel respected you don't work properly. I think that's probably why a lot of people mess about in lessons.

Marion: What about looks?

Tracey: I don't think looks are very important because if you've got a very slim, sexy female teacher then a lot of the boys are going to persuade themselves that they fancy them and then you're into big, um, problems, because the teacher gets embarrassed and they don't work properly and they always feel under pressure to impress the teacher so they probably, um, do lots of stupid things and it usually ends up in trouble for the teacher and the person. So I don't really think looks are very important, as long as they're not grotesquely ugly or something! [laughter]

Laura: Well, obviously, you're not going to have to be Miss World 1982 or whatever it is, but you've got to be, I think, I mean if you are really ugly the, the pupils are not going to be terribly nice to you, are they? I mean they're going to, they're going to teasing you, tease you and take the mickey out of you, and things like that. I don't think looks are very important, but you've not got to be a Hunchback of Notre Dame or anything like that. [laughter]

Marion: And what about age? Do you think there's an ideal age for a teacher?

Laura: Yes, I don't think you ought to be too old because people, I don't know why but I always seem to, I don't seem to respect older teachers so much, I don't know why, I just, but I don't think you ought to be too young because pupils think you're incapable of teaching you properly and they take advantage of the fact.

Tracey: I think they ought to be about thirty, because if they're too old, then um they've been to school ages ago when everything was very strict and, um, they seem to think that everything should be the same, I think it's usually the older teachers that are going to give you a clip round the ear, or give you lines or something. Um, teachers that are too young do, um, they don't have, get respected because if they're just a few years older than us then we're obviously not going to respect them any more than we would each other, so I think about thirty, when, um, they've been to school recently enough to know what to expect of modern schools, but so that they do know also how to control people of today, because we are difficult I think, probably. [laughter]

Time: 4' 15"

UNIT 7

YOUNG ENTERPRISE, Part 1

Geoffrey Harding is the former Director General of Young Enterprise. In this interview he talks about how a Young Enterprise company is set up.

GH: Well, a group of erm young people, twenty to twenty-five in number, of both sexes from various schools would meet once a week starting in September, for two hours on the premises of a sponsor company. A sponsor company is a company that provides the space and facilities for the group of young people and also three or four business executives, who will help the young people run their company. Once they've actually met, the first three or four weeks is a very frenetic erm, full-of-action period. The first thing they do is to erm decide on the name of the company and to elect their managing director, company secretary and accountant. Having chosen the er top directors, and I should say at this stage incidentally that a Young Enterprise company is quite different from any other, in the sense that every young person in the company is a director because he or she buys one share to the value of 25p, which qualifies him or her to be a director of his own company. Having chosen the board of directors, they then decide what products they're going to make in week two of the programme. Now they do this in a brainstorming session by writing a long list of erm ideas up on a blackboard. The average group of twenty or twenty-five young people in about half an hour will come up with between fifty and a hundred ideas, ranging from ludicrous things like nuclear bombs down to basic erm low cost products like jewellery erm and erm cuddly toys.

Marion: And while they're doing all this, is there an adviser present at every meeting?

GH: The advisers, who are specialists in the areas of production, marketing, and accountancy mainly, erm, do attend every meeting wherever possible, particularly in the first three or four weeks when the young people are, are pretty inexperienced at running their company, but once they have erm understood the rudiments of, of running a company, which usually comes after three or four weeks, they tend to take over the total control of their own company.

Marion: What are some of the problems that some of the companies have faced?

GH: The type of problems that the young people face are exactly the type of problems that erm adults face in the real world of business. They will tend to jump in, for instance, and make the wrong type of product before they've done any market research, erm, because it sounds a good idea at the time, and they will do insufficient market research and find, for instance that they overprice their product and they can't sell enough, they will erm do the reverse and underprice their product and of course create a demand which they can't satisfy; they will have industrial relations problems whereby certain young people erm do not pull their weight, (and) play about when they meet and this will c, lead to dismissals from the company, the youngsters will have to meet as a board of directors and make, erm, dismiss certain ineffective Achievers, erm, they will have strike situations over the wage and salary structure, erm, whereby the production workers, who are not erm executive erm directors, erm will get bored and will not be satisfied with a payment each week erm in terms of wages of less than the managing director, so you could have a strike on your hands. They will face all the problems, cash flow problems, product problems, product diversification problems, erm, labour disputes, erm, market erm research problems, quality control problems, all the same sort of challenges that business executives face every day of their working lives in, in, in big business.

Marion: And if at the, at the end of the period,

when the company goes into liquidation, if they've been financially a failure, isn't this a very discouraging experience for them?

GH: The main emphasis on the programme throughout the two terms or eight months when the young people meet is the learning experience. The whole point of the programme is to introduce the young people to the basic concepts of how you run companies, how business is operated and what the various roles are in, in the businesses, so that in fact they will have a better understanding of the adult world when they enter into it, and they'll have a more informed choice of career. But very few companies actually do not erm break even the [maj . . .] vast majority of companies, seventy or eighty per cent, make a healthy profit, erm some companies erm turnover runs into two or three thousand pounds, but the average erm Young Enterprise group, its turnover runs into a few hundred pounds. But as I say, at the end of the day the question of profit is important in terms of motivational value, erm, but it is not the main erm emphasis of the programme.

Time: 5' 30" (approx.)

YOUNG ENTERPRISE, Part 2

Here are two Young Achievers, Josh Dalby and Andrew Collins. Their Young Enterprise company produced stationery and toiletry gift sets. Josh begins by describing his job in the company, which went into liquidation a few months ago.

Josh: At the start erm I was elected erm publicity manager and then erm because we found our costs were very high we merged the two jobs of sales and publicity, so I sort of took over both jobs. Erm, as publicity manager, your main job is to get people, especially the market you want to sell to, to know what you're doing and what you're selling and the prices you're selling at. And you've got to do that as quickly as possible. Erm, at the fir . . . at the outset we thought, erm, we'd have a ready market in our own school, Highbury Grove, but erm it proved that people weren't really interested, (e)specially not in the toiletry sets, although we did sell a few stationery sets, so erm at the beginning we relied on Rotary Club orders from local businesses and erm also parents, friends, teachers in the school. Erm, a few months into the scheme, especially around Christmas, we we moved into Highbury Hill, which is a girls' school down the road, and erm we found a much better audience there. We managed to sell quite a number every week. Erm, also we tried other things like parents' evenings in the school, erm, well I organized just stalls to have there, erm, for two purposes, firstly just to tell them what we were doing and secondly to see if we could sell anything to them, which we did on a number of occasions, erm we raised about twenty-five pounds each parents' evening. Erm, other things, at school fêtes or school jumble sales we had stalls or perhaps even at jumble sales outside the school. Erm, also part of my job was to set the prices of what we were selling. Erm obviously if the price was too high, people wouldn't buy it, which we found out very quickly, because erm we started out with prices around two pounds for each set and erm we soon had to drop that to one fifty and then to one forty-nine. And erm at that price we seemed to sell quite well. Erm, but the main job for publicity and sales is to make sure you sell enough to keep the company going and erm if you don't then to sort out why you're not selling.

Marion: And you Andrew, you were a production manager. [Mhm] Could you tell me about your job?

Andrew: Yeah, well, I was basically responsible for erm planning and execution of the pr, erm, of making the product. Erm, I had a design team of two who would erm who designed the layout of the production room and the – initially they decided on what the product was going to be, layout of the product. Erm, I then had to erm approve what they had given me and then I had to present it to the, the board for erm confirmation. Then I had to have a, ask for a b, have a budget. I had worked out for the first erm three months, it was a hundred pounds and then as much as necessary for the remainder of the company. One of my chief difficulties was to, erm getting enough made in time for Josh to get out to fulfil his orders. Erm, another difficulty I encountered was actually getting supplies in, (e)specially in the winter period, December, January, when there was heavy snow etcetera.

Marion: What do you feel that you learned from the experience? Andrew?

Andrew: I think it was the way, it was handling people, well, not so much outsiders but people actually getting them to do something which you wanted them to do. Erm, not going in, charging in and saying 'You do so and so and so and so' or, or 'You do this and that', you speak to them not not necessarily gently but firmly, but erm convince them that it's a necessary job and that it should be done, if not, so and so will happen and invariably you got, got results. That taught me really how to erm work, taught me also how to work with others, not on a level such as in school but erm on a ordinary work to work, erm working level, sort of thing, to work with others. Erm, how to behave responsibly, not muck about sort of thing, you . . . you cos you know erm if you do, then you know that erm everything you've done and worked for is going to go down the drain. Erm, it taught taught me erm the art of good communications, that was pretty vital. Erm, if, if erm communi . . . erm even a slight break in communications i.e. erm transport, ordinary just getting in contact with somebody else or, or just talking to somebody else it could foul up a whole evening's work, and that was, that did prove erm and that and that was proved on a number of occasions.

Marion: And what do you think you learned, Josh?

Josh: Um, yeah, I'd like to agree with Andrew there. I think erm learning to work with other people in the company was, erm I think the biggest challenge and erm the thing I've most gained out of it, I think. Erm because at the beginning I was one of those that said all the decisions we took, even the smallest ones, should be decided on and voted by and agreed by everyone in the company. But erm I think towards the end I started realizing that the people who are elected by the company to take the decisions should be allowed to get on with it as long as they take reasonable decisions, erm, because it was just, it proved impractical to sort of discuss everything, especially as we only had two hours together erm one evening every week. Erm, apart from that though I think I've learned about the jobs that different people do, for instance production and accountants, which I wouldn't really have known about before, and erm, I've learned about how a company moves along, for instance you start with the budget, and then you've got to realize, like you've got to take into account your expenses and overheads and wages and erm, it was interesting to see how high you can set wages to keep everyone happy without upsetting the balance of the cash flow.

Time: 6′ 10″ (approx.)

UNIT 8

DRIVE AN AD!

Marion: David, could you tell me what Poster Motors is?

David Barnes: Yes, Poster Motors is advertising erm all over cars. And er the way we do it is we recruit a fleet of mini owners, erm, and we then decorate those cars in the livery of the advertiser.

Marion: And why do you choose this kind of advertising rather than for example television commercials?

David Barnes: Well, there are many many reasons, one of which could be that the advertiser can't afford television. It's a very expensive medium, erm, it may not be necessary to use television and erm all its educational qualities. It may just be that they want to run a straight branding exercise, i.e. get their product name over at, on a top-of-the-mind level. Erm, that's just one of the reasons of course.

Marion: And how much do you pay people to paint their cars?

David Barnes: Not a lot. Erm, we first of all, we paint their cars. Erm, when we decorate the cars all the cars are sprayed in the same base colour of the advertiser's choice before the design is put on to the car and that's in the form of vinyl decal. Erm, we pay people six pounds a month plus a ten pound bonus at the end of a six month period. Erm, it's not a lot of money, erm, people don't do it for the money, they do it because they enjoy doing it.

Marion: But what sort of people enjoy doing it?

David Barnes: All sorts. Absolutely all sorts. We've had grannies, erm, Stirling Moss has telephoned us, erm, in the early days offering his Volkswagen Dormobile van to be done. We've had five people with Rolls Royces wanting their cars done. Erm, so all sorts, grannies, erm, younger people, teenagers, erm married women, women with children.

Marion: And do you do Rolls Royces or is it only minis?

David Barnes: No, we don't actually. I, I don't think the advertisers could afford to spray them, erm, and besides I would hate to see a Rolls Royce charge around with advertising on it. Erm, there are very good reasons why we just have Minis. Erm, first of all the, it's a classless car, you can be a duke or a dustman and drive a Mini. Erm, it has a very wide appeal across the ages, for in . . ., as I said grannies drive them, erm, young people drive them, as, as a first car. Erm, an awful lot of them are around the place as well. There are about, I think about two and a half million on the roads in this country and that means we can find the right people with the right cars in the right places for any campaign.

Marion: And why do you think people do like having their cars painted in this way?

David Barnes: Well, it's taken us a long time to find that out. We thought first of all they'd be extroverts coming along, erm, but we found in fact that it seems to be the reverse. The introverted people come along wanting their cars done and perhaps it's a way of getting themselves noticed and erm starting up conversations. Erm . . .

Marion: Are there any special products that lend themselves to this kind of advertising?

David Barnes: I like to think that we have a very wide appeal in terms of product range, different types of products or services that can be advertised. I think perhaps though that because erm inevitably there's a bias towards the younger end of the market in, in terms of Mini cars erm that perhaps, and because it's a new and exciting way of advertising perhaps we lend ourselves best to new exciting products, erm, life style products like jeans for instance.

Marion: And do you operate only in Britain or do you operate in Europe and other countries?

David Barnes: Well, Poster Motors offers the service in the UK and the Republic of Ireland. Erm, sister companies of ours operate it in, or offer the service in West Germany and Denmark. And we have sister companies in I think just about every European country. And they'd be certainly delighted to set something up for anyone who came along. Erm, the system is run in the States by a different company on erm Volkswagen Beetles, with some success.

Time: 4' 10" (approx.)

UNIT 9

WHAT HAS SEX GOT TO DO WITH IT?

One of the most interesting areas of English usage is how we refer to inanimate objects, when we want to give them a personality. When we talk about a country as a political unit, for instance, it's usually referred to as feminine. We say 'England is proud of her history', and never 'England is proud of his history'. Or again, when we refer affectionately to personal possessions, the norm is also feminine. I once heard a stamp collector pick up a specimen and say, 'Isn't she beautiful!' Cars, too, are usually feminine, for both men and women. 'She handles superbly', I heard someone say recently – about his new Rover. Mind you, I do know one woman who insists on referring to her sports car as *he*, and I have a colleague at my University who calls his old car *Fred*, talking about it using masculine pronouns only.

What about animate beings whose sex you don't know? Insects, for instance, whose sex only an expert could determine. They're mainly *it*, of course, especially if they have large numbers of legs. But if you're feeling at all affectionate towards them, the masculine pronouns are generally used. I heard a father telling his young child once, 'Look at him, crawling along there. He's looking for some food.' The object in question was a cockroach.

Then there's the opposite situation. Human beings can be referred to as *it*, even when you do know what sex they are. A baby that cries in unsocial hours, for instance, stands a very good chance of being linguistically neutered. And there are several other cases of this kind. I heard a sixteen-year-old girl telling her friend about the previous evening's disco. She said, 'Robert ignored me all evening, and then it finally asked me to dance.' And I heard a mother leading her filthy five-year-old son in from the garden: she said, 'Look at it! Have you ever seen such a mess!' And then again, at a party, a group of chatty friends contained one quiet member. The quiet one piped up after a while, somewhat unexpectedly, at which point one of the group made the comment, 'It spoke!'

One of the most awkward usage problems arises when you don't want to say whether you're talking about a man or a woman. English doesn't easily let you do this. You can't use *it*, for that could be rude, as you've just heard. The word *one* is a neutral form, but it's appropriate only for very formal situations or personalities, in speech. Many people avoid it, because it reminds them of the excessively formal speech style of some public figures, where 'One fell off one's horse' means 'I fell off my horse'. But if you don't use *one*, you're left with only *he* or *she*. There isn't a nice, comfy, everyday neutral pronoun in English. Not when you're talking about just one person, anyway.

The problem comes to the boil in sentences beginning with a word like *anyone, anybody, someone* or *somebody*. Take a sentence such as 'Anyone can have a drink if he wants'. The use of *he* here is the traditional one. It would be used even if women were part of the 'anyone'. But this usage has been attacked by feminists in recent years, as another example of the male bias of English. So what alternative is there? To replace *he* by *she* wouldn't satisfy anyone. Males wouldn't use it. And females in any case would find it insulting, because of the nuance it can carry. Just listen to 'Anyone can have a drink if she wants'.

Of course, it would be possible to avoid the sexist lobby altogether, by using a compound phrase, such as *he or she*. And this is what is usually done in formal writing – either in full, or in an abbreviated form, such as *s stroke h e*. But it's a really awkward construction in speech. Try saying 'Anyone can have a drink if he or she wants'. The informal way out of the problem has long been to use *they*, with a change of verb from singular to plural. That would produce 'Anyone can have a drink if they want'. No problems with sex there. But unfortunately, this usage is like a red rag to a bull for traditional grammarians, who point to the singular sense of the word *anyone,* and say, 'You can't have a plural *they* referring to a singular *anyone*.' But, needs must . . . And these days, *they* is in fact the commonest way out of the difficulty. It's even finding its way into contexts where it wouldn't have appeared a generation ago without criticism. I've often heard it in questions in formal speech, for instance, where it passes unnoticed. I heard a school quizmaster say, 'Someone should be able to identify the author, shouldn't they?' And I heard a Member of Parliament say, 'Anyone might have found it, mightn't they?'

So at present, there are at least three usages competing for our attention in these sentences: *he*, *he or she* and *they*. There have even been proposals for a brand new pronoun, to get themselves out of the problem. I recall one proposal for *hem*, another for *shay*, and a progressive community in the United States once decided to replace all instances of *he* or *she* by the word *co* – that's *c, o* – an experiment which seems to have petered out after a few days. Some people have suggested resuscitating the old Anglo-Saxon pronoun *mon*, which was sex-neutral. I suppose if you've nothing better to do, thinking up new sex-neutral personal pronouns in English is a way of passing the time. But don't think they'll catch on. If there's to be a permanent language change in this area of English, it'll not come as a consequence of an artificial process of invention. It'll be the result of a long process of unconscious, natural selection. Language change is like that – impossible to predict, but easy to recognize once it's arrived. I can't tell you what set of forms will win. But if you dig this recording out of the archives in 100 years time – you'll know.

Time: 5' 35" (approx.)